You Can Teach Yourself® Tinwhistle

By Mizzy McCaskill & Dona Gilliam

D1353417

Cathel

CD CONTENTS*

*This book is available as a book only or as a book/compact disc configuration.

1 2 3 4 5 6 7 8 9 0

Visit us on the Web at www.melbay.com — E-mail us at email@melbay.com

THE MUSIC SHOP
TEL 01463 233374
£15-99

Index of Songs

A Word About the Whistle . . .

The tin whistle is a versatile and easy-to-play folk instrument. It is a member of the vertical fipple flute family: vertical—it is held in a vertical position; fipple—a block in the windway that splits the air stream across the tube thereby creating a sound; and flute—it uses the breath blown into a tube to create sound. Tin whistles are also referred to as penny whistles: penny—a reference to the original low cost of the instrument in the British Isles; and tin—because certain makers form the body of the instrument from tin.

The tin whistle is a popular Irish folk instrument and a standard member of many Irish folk groups. Irish musicians often begin their musical training on the humble whistle before switching to the flute or uilleann pipes. The whistle has extended far beyond the Irish folk domain due to its appealing tone quality and ease of mastery. It adapts well to the folk music of many cultures, and is now played by amateur and professional musicians around the world.

Hand Position:

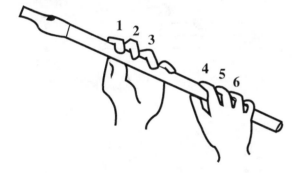

Cover the top three tone holes with the first three fingers of the left hand.

Cover the bottom three tone holes with the first three fingers of the right hand.

Instrument rests on thumbs.

To Sound:

Sit up straight. Take a normal breath. Move tongue as if saying 'too' while blowing a steady stream of air.

Musical Facts

The sequential method presented in this book requires familiarity with written notation. Review the following musical facts and carefully listen to the accompanimental cassette to assure accuracy of pitch and rhythm.

Staff

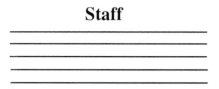

The **staff** consists of the 5 lines and 4 spaces upon which notes are placed.

Treble Clef

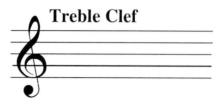

The **treble clef** or **G clef** is placed at the beginning of a staff. It indicates the pitch of the notes to follow because it circles the G line.

Note Names

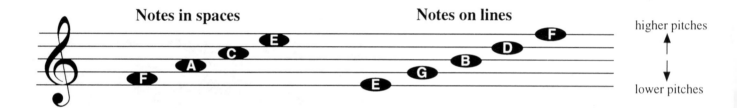

When pitches exceed the range of five staff lines they are notated with the use of **leger lines**. **Leger lines** are short lines added above or below the staff.

For example:

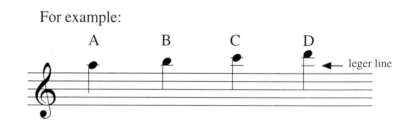

Notational Terms

Notes and note groups are comprised of various parts:

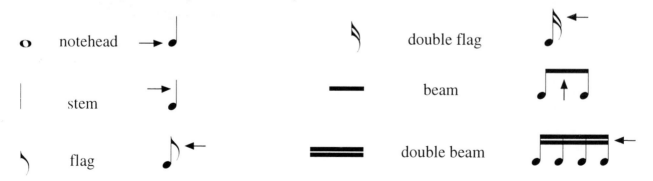

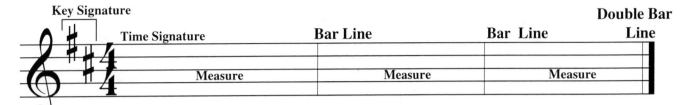

Bar Lines are used to divide the staff into measures. The space between bar lines is called a **measure**. The **double bar line** is used at the end of a musical selection.

Key Signature

Key Signature for **D**

This book is written for a tin whistle pitched in D (when all of the tone holes are covered the note D sounds). The key of D Major has two sharps (#) noted in the key signature—F sharp and C sharp.

Although the whistle is pitched in D it can be played in other keys. The keys of G Major and A Major are also represented in this book:

Key Signature for **G**    **Key Signature** for **A**

Time Signature

4	3	2	Top number tells how many counts in a measure.	6	9
4	4	4	Bottom number tells what kind of a note receives one count.	8	8

(quarter note receives one count)   (eighth note receives one count)

Note Values

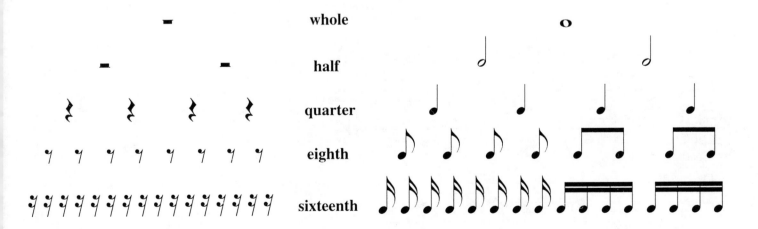

First Note B

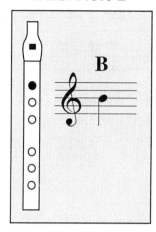

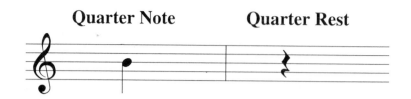

The **quarter note** receives **one** count.

The **quarter rest** receives **one** count.

Exercise 1

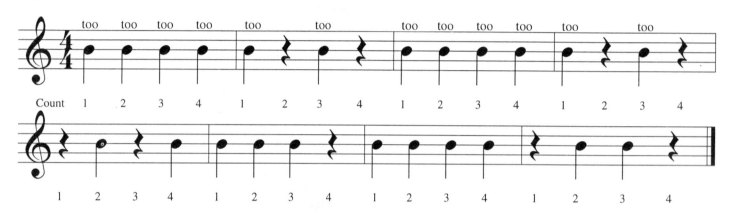

Exercise 2

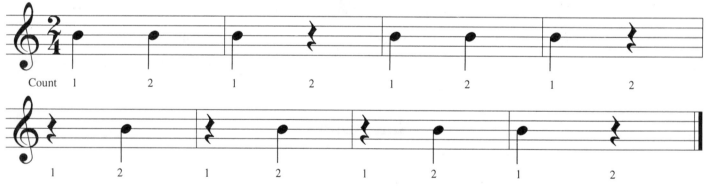

Exercise 3

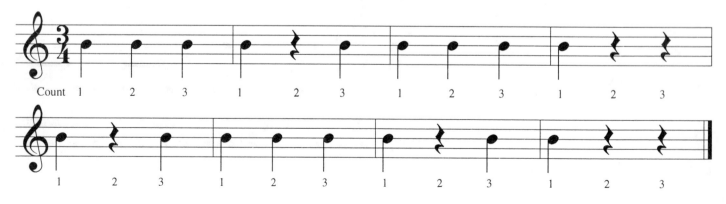

New Note A

New Note A

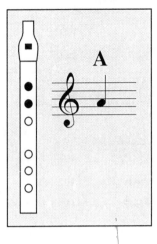

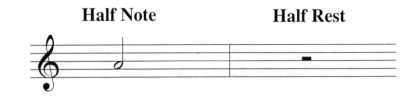

Half Note   **Half Rest**

The **half note** receives **two** counts.

The **half rest** receives **two** counts.

Exercise 1

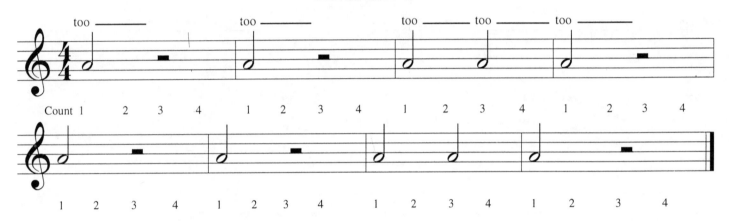

Exercise 2

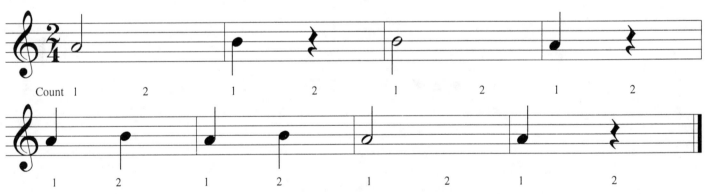

Exercise 3

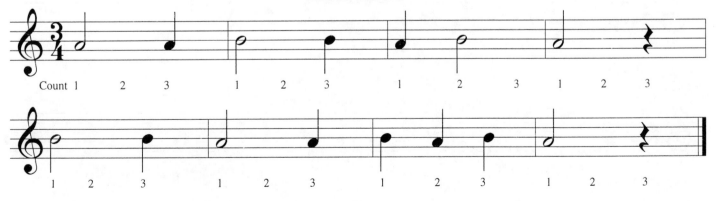

New Note G

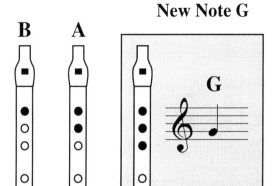

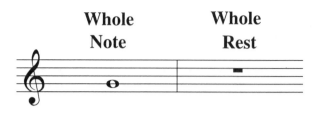

The **whole note** receives **four** counts.

The **whole rest** receives **four** counts.
Notice that the **whole rest** hangs from the line.

Exercise 1

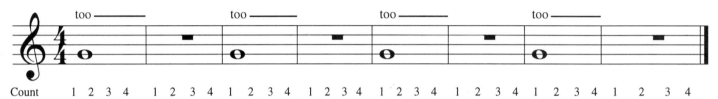

Exercise 2

Exercise 3

8

Songs Using B, A and G

Merrily We Roll Along

Hot Cross Buns

Fais Do Do

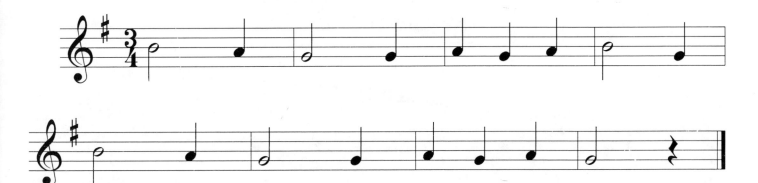

Songs Using B, A and G

Au Clair de la Lune

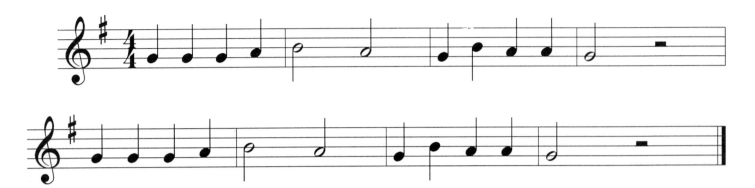

Cuckoo

New Note C Sharp

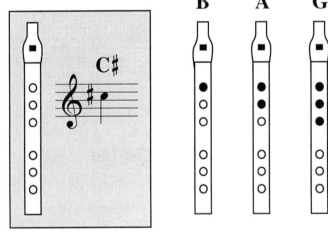

Exercise 1

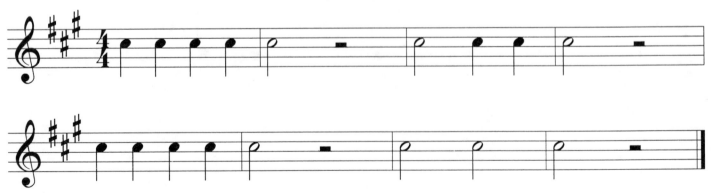

Songs/Exercise Using C Sharp

Exercise 2

Common Time

C is a symbol for **common time**, and is a substitute for $\frac{4}{4}$ time.

Merrily We Roll Along

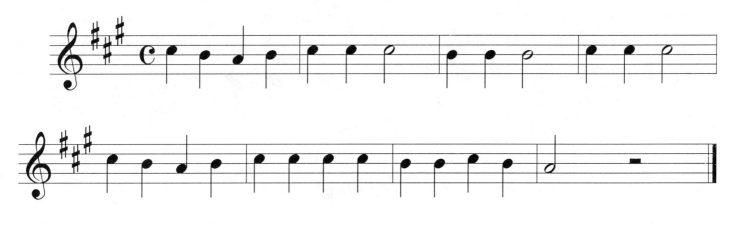

Hot Cross Buns

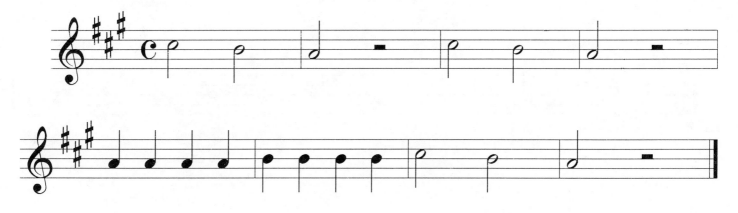

Au Clair de la Lune

Fais Do Do

Cuckoo

New Note F Sharp

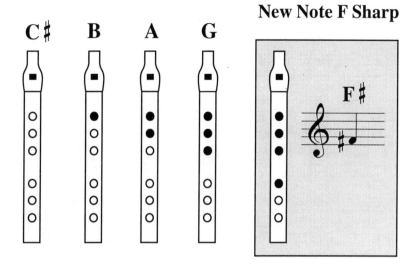

Exercise 1

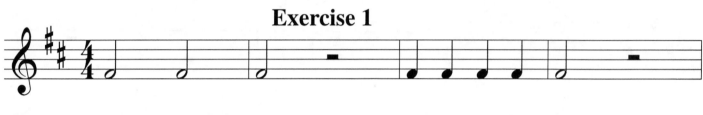

Dotted Half Note

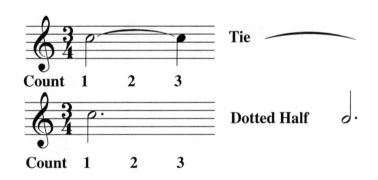

Tie

A **tie** is a curved line connecting two notes of the same pitch. They are played as one note.

Dotted Half

The **dot** is equal to one half the value of the note it follows. In this example

Exercise 2

New Note E

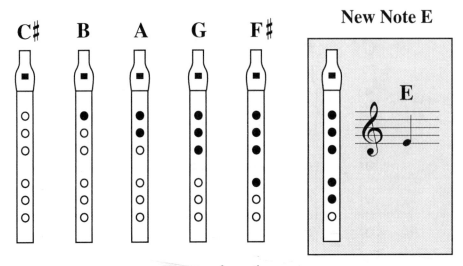

Exercise 1

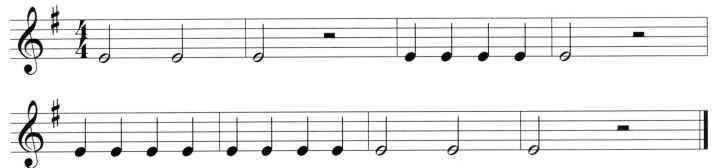

Round

A **round** is a song in which two or more groups play the same melody starting at different times.

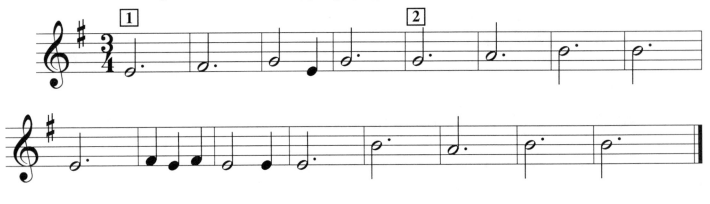

Exercise 2

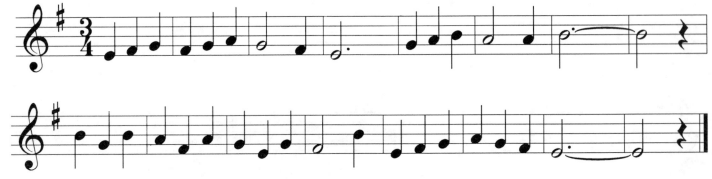

Pick-Up Notes

The following piece begins on the last count of a measure. This note is called a **pick-up note**. When a piece begins with one or more pick-up notes the last measure of the piece will be shortened by the value of the pick-up note(s).

Exercise Using Pick-up Note

New Note C Natural

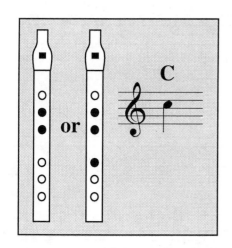

When the key signature (shown at the beginning of each staff line) does not show C sharp (C#), the player must use **C natural (C ♮)** throughout the piece. Always check the key signature before playing, as many of the following pieces use C natural.

Two different fingerings are shown for C natural.
Use the fingering that sounds best on your instrument.

C Natural Exercise 1

15

More Exercises Using C Natural

Exercise 2

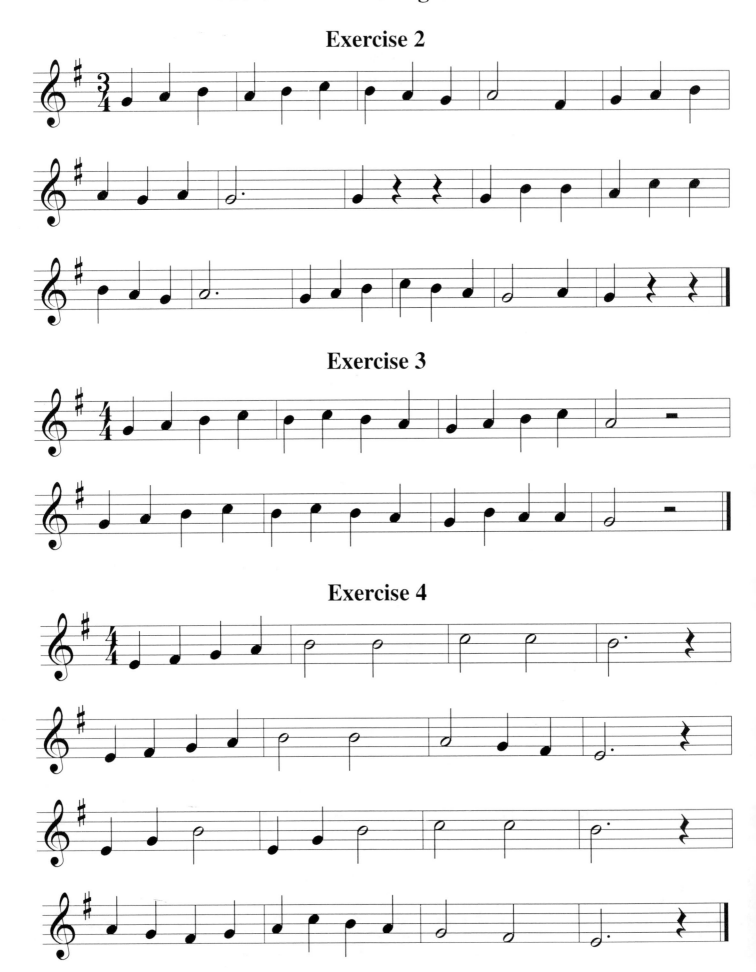

Exercise 3

Exercise 4

New Note Low D

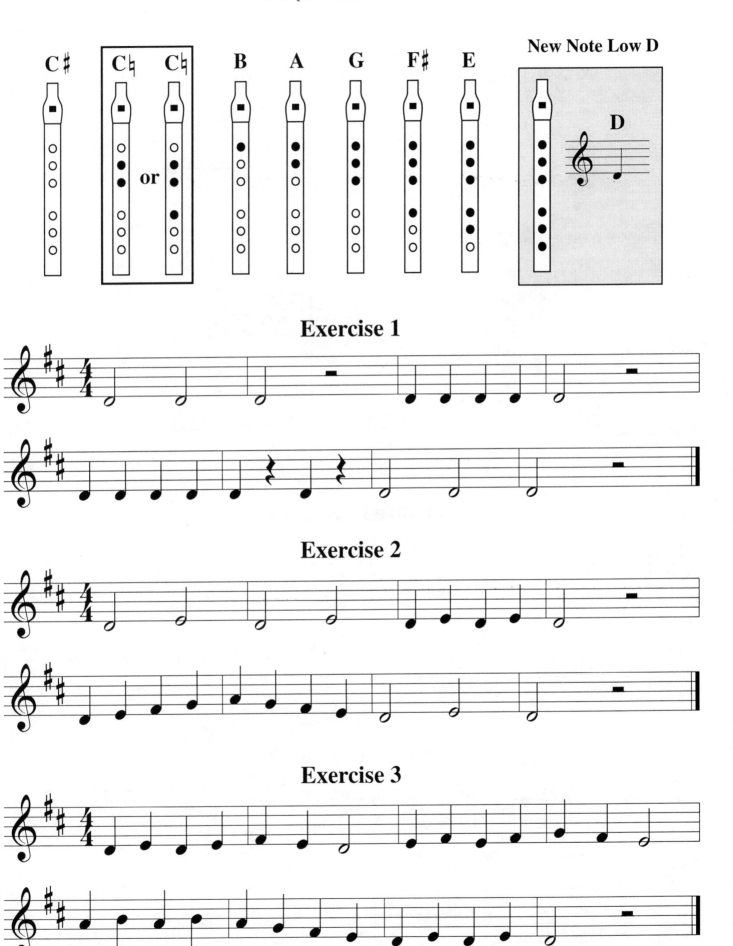

Exercise 1

Exercise 2

Exercise 3

17

New Note High D

Each fingering on the whistle will produce a low or high note depending upon the speed of the player's air stream. Low D and High D are one **octave** apart.

Low D

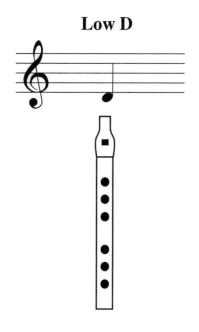

Blow **softly** to play **low** D.

High D

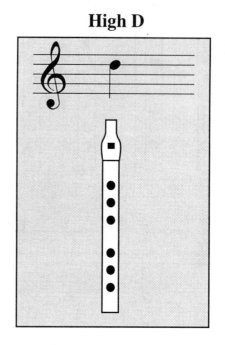

Blow a **fast** air stream to play **high** D.

Octave Exercise 1

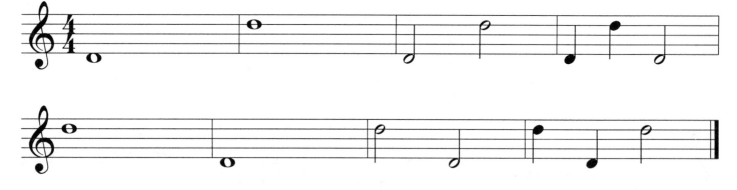

Octave Exercise 2

Exercise/Song Using Low D

Fingering Review

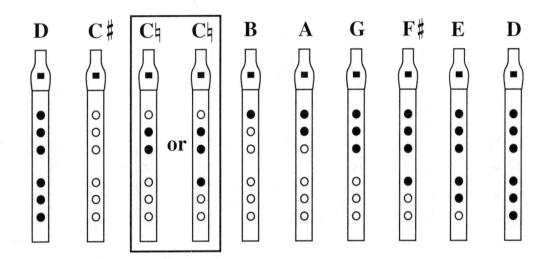

Exercise 1

When the Saints Go Marching In

Spiritual

D Major Scale

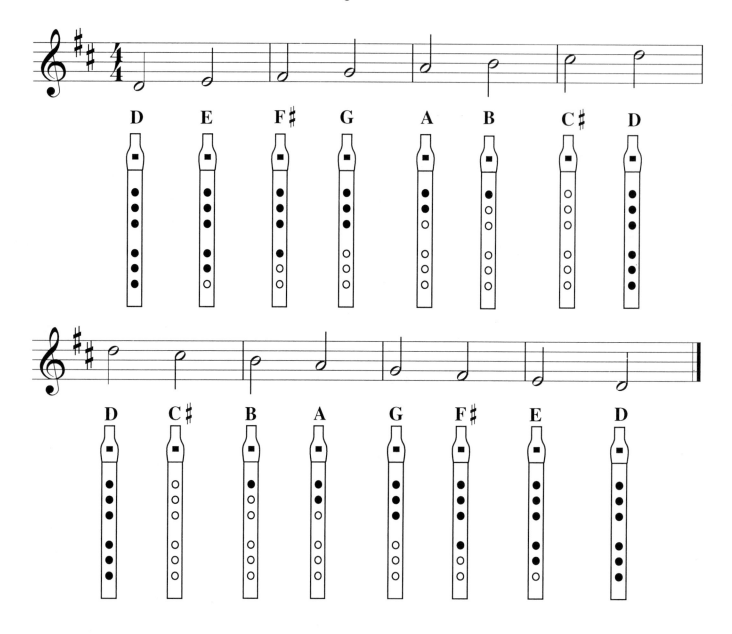

Scale Exercise 1

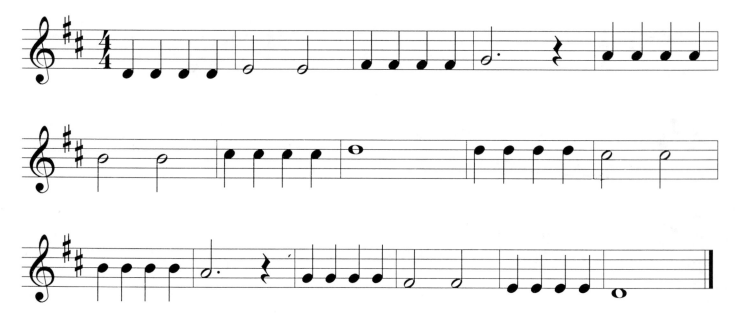

Scale Exercise 2

Playing Tips

1. Each fingering on the whistle will produce a low or high note depending upon the speed of the player's air stream. Blow softly to play low notes. Blow a faster air stream to play high notes. A steady air stream will allow you to control low and high registers with ease.

2. Tongue the beginning of each note as if you are whispering the word 'too' (unless the note is under a slur or tie). This will assure a crisp, clear attack for every note.

3. If you have difficulty making certain notes sound on the whistle check for air leaking beneath the pads of the fingers. This problem can be corrected by careful attention to proper finger and hand position.

4. Keep a relaxed hand position, and try to avoid excess tension caused by gripping the whistle with a tighter hold than necessary. A relaxed hand position will allow you to play fast passages with ease.

5. Should moisture form in the windway and prevent notes from sounding, remove moisture by sealing the fipple opening with a finger and blowing a fast stream of air into the instrument.

Daisy Bell

Harry Dacre

Repeat Signs

Repeat signs indicate that music between the two signs is to be repeated. If only one repeat sign is used return to the beginning.

When I Was a Young Girl

English Folk

The Keys of Canterbury

English Folk

As I Was Going to Banbury

English Folk

Cut Time

¢ is a symbol for **cut time**, *alla breve*, or fast double time. The sign indicates that the half note becomes the basic pulse (beat) for each measure rather than the quarter note. If the switch to cut time impedes your playing progress simply beat a fast 𝄴 time.

The Red River Valley

American Folk

Rigaudon

Jacques Hotteterre (1738)

Chanukah, Chanukah

Traditional

Good King Wenceslas

Traditional

First and Second Endings

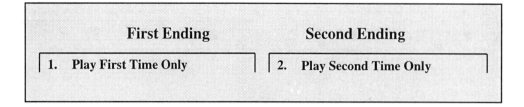

First Ending	Second Ending
1. Play First Time Only	2. Play Second Time Only

The Sidewalks of New York

James W. Blake
& Charles B. Lawlor

26

Eighth Notes

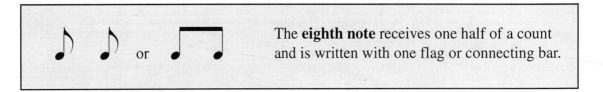

The **eighth note** receives one half of a count and is written with one flag or connecting bar.

Use the quarter note beat when counting eighth notes, and divide each beat into equal parts.

Count   1   &   2   &   3   &   4   &

Eighth Note Exercise

Count 1 & 2 & 3 & 4   1 & 2 & 3 & 4 &

Sweet Betsy from Pike

English Melody

28

Yellow Rose of Texas

J.K. (1858)

El Coqui

Puerto Rican Folk

Shady Grove

American Folk

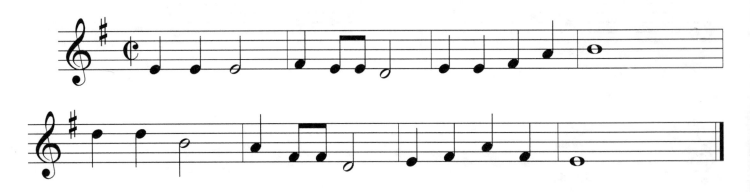

Minuet

J.S. Bach

Jolly Old Saint Nicholas

Traditional

Dotted Quarter Note

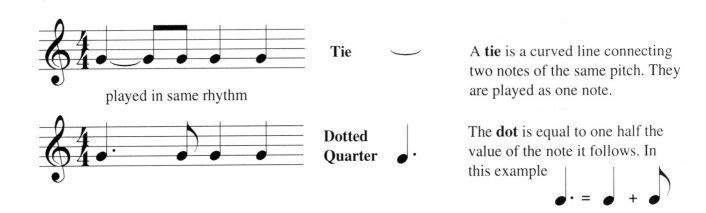

played in same rhythm

Tie

A **tie** is a curved line connecting two notes of the same pitch. They are played as one note.

Dotted Quarter

The **dot** is equal to one half the value of the note it follows. In this example

I Ride an Old Paint

Cowboy Song

My Home is in Montana

Cowboy Song

Sarasponda

Dutch Folk Song

33

Accidentals

The note C natural is used as an **accidental** in the following piece. Accidentals are signs used in musical notation to alter pitches indicated by the key signature. In this piece the **natural sign** (♮) is used to indicate that C natural should be played rather than C sharp. An accidental affects all notes of the same pitch and octave within the same measure. A bar line cancels the accidental.

Whoopee Ti Yi Yo

Cowboy Song

Home Sweet Home

Henry R. Bishop

Amazing Grace

American Folk Hymn

Believe Me All Those Endearing Young Charms

Irish

Marine's Hymn

Melody from Jacques Offenbach's
Geneviève de Brabant

Michael, Row the Boat Ashore

Spiritual

Syncopation

Syncopation describes the displacement of accented notes in normal metric notation.

Familiar folk melodies are most often constructed in metrical groups of two or three, with regularly recurring accents on the first beat of each group. For example:

Syncopation occurs when emphasis is placed on weaker or unaccented beats in a measure. For example:

The following song uses syncopated rhythms.

Buffalo Gals

American Folk

Oh, dem Golden Slippers

James Bland

New Note High E

Each fingering on the whistle will produce a low or high note depending upon the speed of the player's air stream. Low E and High E are one **octave** apart.

Low E

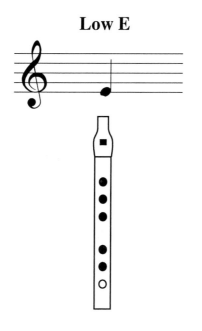

Blow **softly** to play **low** E.

High E

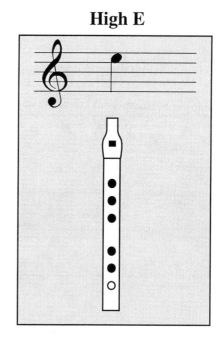

Blow a **fast** air stream to play **high** E.

Octave Exercise 1

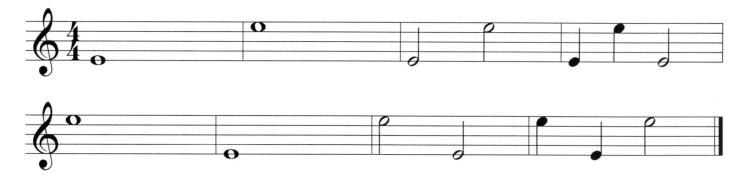

Octave Exercise 2

Cindy

American Folk

Crawdad Song

American Folk

All Through the Night

Welsh

Auld Lang Syne

Scottish Air

The Caissons Go Rolling Along

Edmund L. Gruber

Did You Ever See a Lassie?

German

Swing Low, Sweet Chariot

Spiritual

The British Grenadiers

English

Ties, Slurs, and Phrase Markings

Tie ——— A tie is a curved line connecting two notes of the **same** pitch. They are played as one note.

tie

Slur ⌣ A slur is a curved line connecting notes of **different** pitch. Tongue only the first note of a slur.

slur   slur   slur

Phrase - A phrase marking in music is similar to a sentence in prose. It indicates a complete musical thought, and is used to give structure and continuity to the performance of a tune. Phrases often follow the text of a song, hence phrase markings can be used as appropriate places to take a breath without interrupting the musical line.

phrase

Classical themes are often performed on the whistle when the range and keys are suitable for the instrument. Following are two well-known orchestral themes.

German composer Johannes Brahms wrote *Honor Bound* for the fourth movement of his Symphony No. 1. The lyrical, and striking melody has given it lasting appeal.

Honor Bound

Johannes Brahms

Finnish composer Jean Sibelius wrote the following theme for his symphonic poem *Finlandia*. The melody was written during a time when Finland was seeking independence from Russia in the nineteenth century, and it has since become a national 'folk anthem' of Finland.

Theme from *Finlandia*

Jean Sibelius

New Note High F Sharp

Each fingering on the whistle will produce a low or high note depending upon the speed of the player's air stream. Low F# and High F# are one **octave** apart.

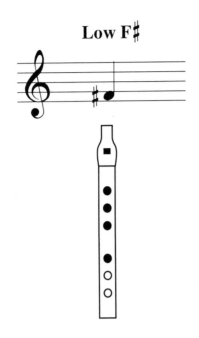

Low F♯

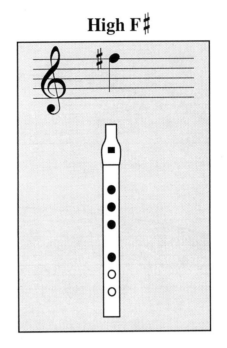

High F♯

Blow **softly** to play **low F#**.

Blow a **fast** air stream to play **high F#**.

Octave Exercise 1

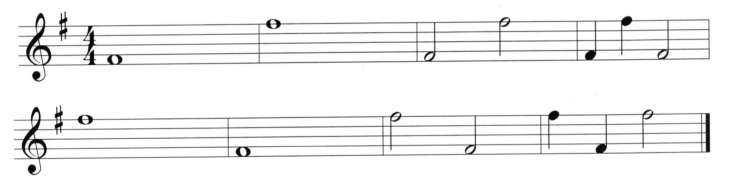

Octave Exercise 2

High Octave Practice

Fais Do Do

Merry Widow Waltz

Franz Lehár

In the Good Old Summertime

George Evans

My Bonnie Lies Over the Ocean

American Folk

New Note High G

Each fingering on the whistle will produce a low or high note depending upon the speed of the player's air stream. Low G and High G are one **octave** apart.

Low G

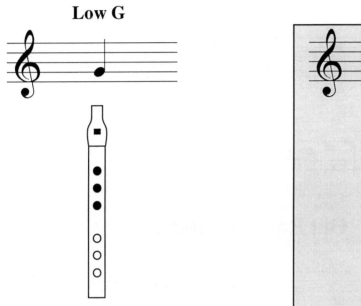

Blow **softly** to play **low** G.

High G

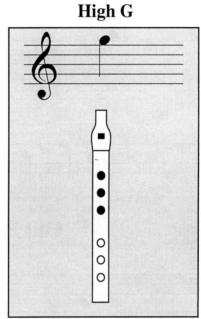

Blow a **fast** air stream to play **high** G.

G Major Scale

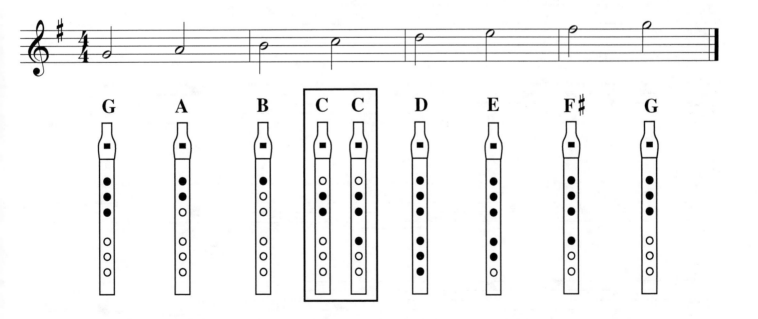

She'll Be Comin' Round the Mountain

American Folk

Old Rosin the Beau

Irish

Hail to the Chief

Traditional

My Wild Irish Rose

Chauncey Olcott

The Wearin' o' the Green

Irish

Sixteenth Notes

Rest Values		Note Values
	whole	
	half	
	quarter	
	eighth	
	sixteenth	

Skip to My Lou

Traditional

59

Black Dance

Beck (1786)

Little Brown Jug

American Folk

God Save the King

English

Dotted Eighth Note

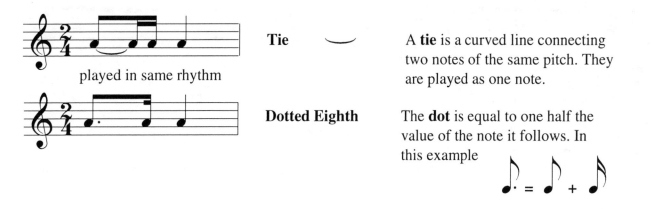

played in same rhythm

Tie — A **tie** is a curved line connecting two notes of the same pitch. They are played as one note.

Dotted Eighth — The **dot** is equal to one half the value of the note it follows. In this example

Clementine

American Folk

Alouette

French-Canadian Folk

Aloha Oe

Queen Liliuokalani (Hawaii)

Erie Canal

American Folk

Half Hole/New Note G Sharp

New Note G Sharp

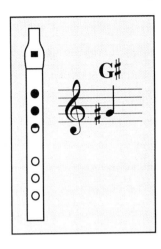

Half Hole Symbol

The G# fingering uses a half hole on the third finger of the left hand. The half hole is formed (as its name implies) by sliding the finger forward or drawing the finger back until it covers only half of the tone hole.

The note G# is used as an **accidental** in the following two pieces. Accidentals are signs used in musical notation to alter pitches indicated by the key signature. Note that G# is not found in the key signature of the following two pieces. An accidental affects all notes of the same pitch and octave within the same measure. A bar line cancels the accidental.

The Yankee Doodle Boy

George M. Cohan

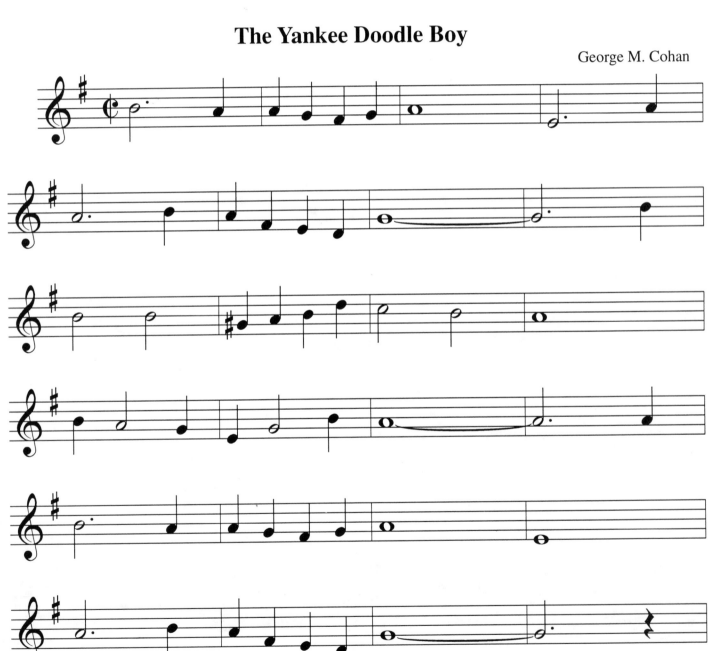

When Irish Eyes Are Smiling

Ernest R. Ball

New Note High A

Each fingering on the whistle will produce a low or high note depending upon the speed of the player's air stream. Low A and High A are one **octave** apart.

Low A

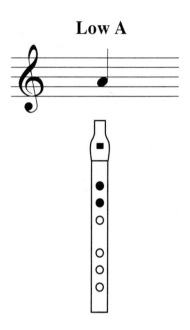

Blow **softly** to play **low** A.

High A

Blow a **fast** air stream to play **high** A.

A Major Scale

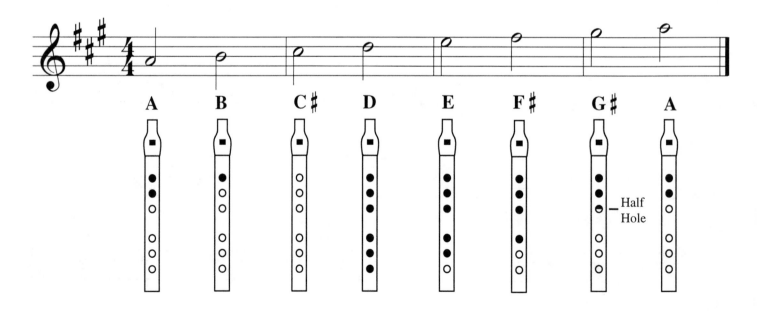

A   B   C♯   D   E   F♯   G♯   A

Half Hole

Grandfather's Clock

Henry Clay Work

Reuben and Rachel

William Gooch

Sourwood Mountain

American Folk

Compound Time

Compound time signatures are those in which the strong counts are subdivided by three.

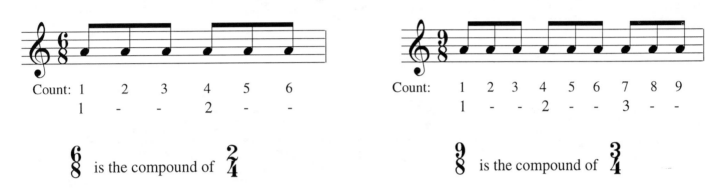

$\frac{6}{8}$, $\frac{9}{8}$ Top number tells how many counts in a measure
Bottom number tells what kind of note receives one count (eighth note)

Count: 1   2   3   4   5   6
      1   -   -   2   -   -

Count: 1 2 3 4 5 6 7 8 9
      1 - - 2 - - 3 - -

$\frac{6}{8}$ is the compound of $\frac{2}{4}$

$\frac{9}{8}$ is the compound of $\frac{3}{4}$

Vive la Compagnie

Folk

Captain Jinks

Irish

I Saw Three Ships

English

Rio Grande

Sea Chantey

Extending the Range

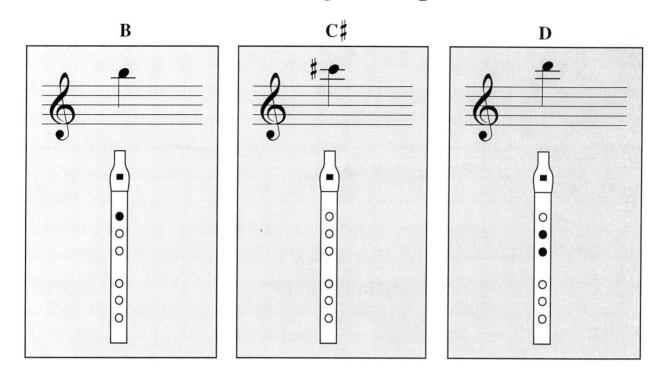

Octave Exercise

Two Octave Scale

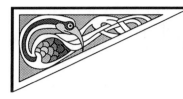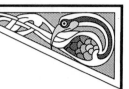

Irish Music

The tin whistle is a folk instrument of Irish origin. The traditional Irish style of whistle playing involves ornamentation of basic tunes, and the best way to learn appropriate ornamentation is to study recorded examples of players who have mastered the instrument. Following is a basic vocabulary of ornaments used by traditional players. Keep in mind that individual playing styles vary, and that there is no one correct way to ornament a tune.

Irish Ornamentation

Slide - The **slide** is performed by gradually sliding the finger off of the tone hole beneath the principal note until the notated pitch sounds.

Triplet - A **triplet** consists of three notes played in the time of two notes. It is used to fill a space in between notes (Example A), or to add more motion to a section of music (Examples B, and C).

Vibrato - **Vibrato** is a fluctuation of pitch used on sustained notes. It is used as a means of musical expression. Traditional whistle players make use of a fingered vibrato, i.e. a vibrato that is created by rapidly tapping one or more fingers on at least one tone hole below the last covered hole. This type of vibrato is used on the notes b, a, g, and f#. Experiment on your whistle to achieve the fingering combination that will best represent the desired effect.

Cut - The **cut** is a grace note, or a note played quickly before the principal note. Tongue only the first note of the ornament. Cuts on the notes d, e, f, and g are produced by fingering the principal note and lifting the third finger of the left hand. Cuts on the notes a and b are produced by fingering the principal note and lifting the first finger of the left hand. (Other fingerings are possible for cuts. Experiment to find the fingerings on your instrument that will produce the desired effect and facilitate ease in playing.)

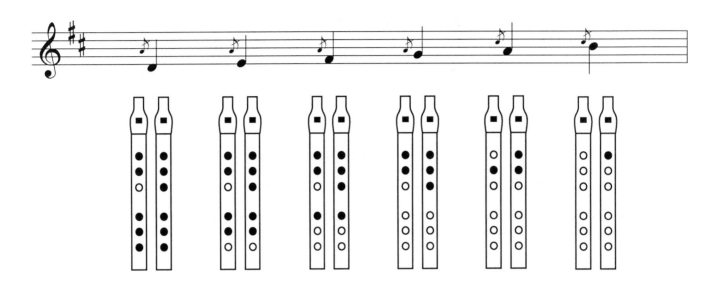

Double Grace - The **double grace** figure consists of two grace notes played quickly before the principal note. Tongue only the first note of the ornament. The upper grace note uses the same fingering as the cut (shown above).

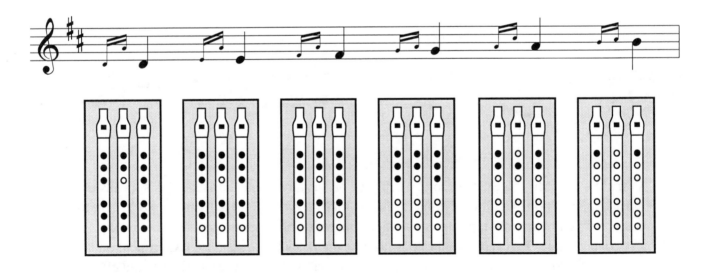

Short Roll - The **short roll** is played by cutting above the principal note and 'tipping' below the principal note. Tongue only the first note of the ornament. Cuts are fingered as shown on the previous page, while tipped notes are played with normal fingerings.

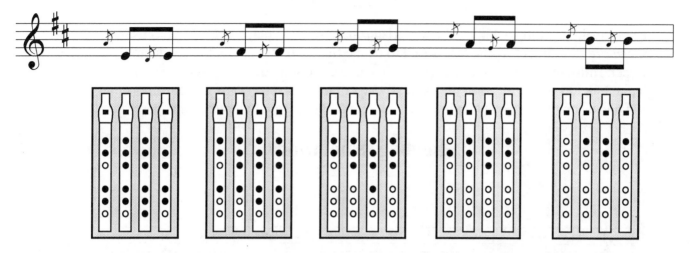

Short rolls are often notated with the curved symbol shown below.

Long Roll - The **long roll** begins on the principal note of the ornament and is cut and tipped in the same manner as the short roll. Tongue only the first note of the ornament.

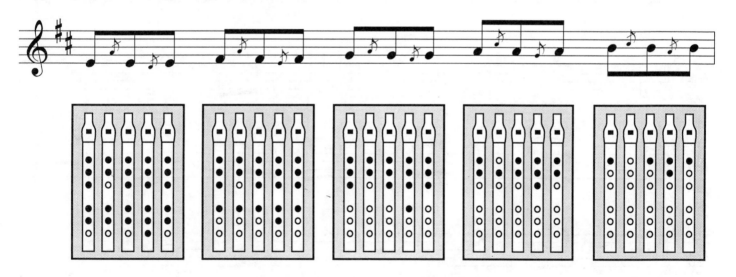

Long rolls are also notated with the curved symbol shown below.

The lyrical, haunting melodies of many Irish songs are often played as solo pieces. *Sheebeg Sheemore* is an Irish favorite that is said to be the first song written by the legendary Irish harper Turlough Carolan. The player should capture the song tradition when playing this tune, and attempt to play with all of the expressive qualities of a singer. The use of ornamentation will add a songlike character to the tune, especially the fingered vibrato and slides.

Sheebeg, Sheemore

Irish Air

Dance Tunes

Jig

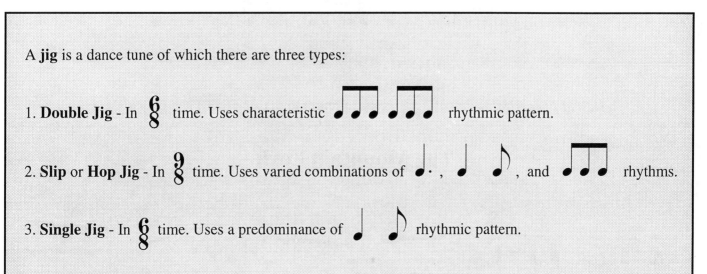

A **jig** is a dance tune of which there are three types:

1. **Double Jig** - In $\frac{6}{8}$ time. Uses characteristic ♪♪♪ ♪♪♪ rhythmic pattern.

2. **Slip** or **Hop Jig** - In $\frac{9}{8}$ time. Uses varied combinations of ♪. , ♪ ♪ , and ♪♪♪ rhythms.

3. **Single Jig** - In $\frac{6}{8}$ time. Uses a predominance of ♩♪ rhythmic pattern.

Kesh Jig

Irish

Reel

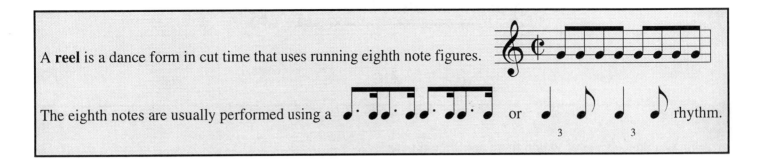

A **reel** is a dance form in cut time that uses running eighth note figures.

The eighth notes are usually performed using a ... or ... rhythm.

D.S. al Fine - Dal Segno al Fine means to return to the sign (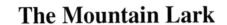) and play to the *Fine*.

The Mountain Lark

Irish

Hornpipe

The **hornpipe** is a dance form in common time that is played at a slower tempo than the reel. Performance practice dictates a pronounced accent on the first and third beat of a hornpipe, and although it is notated using running eighth note figures it is performed using a  rhythm.

The Boys of Bluehill

Irish

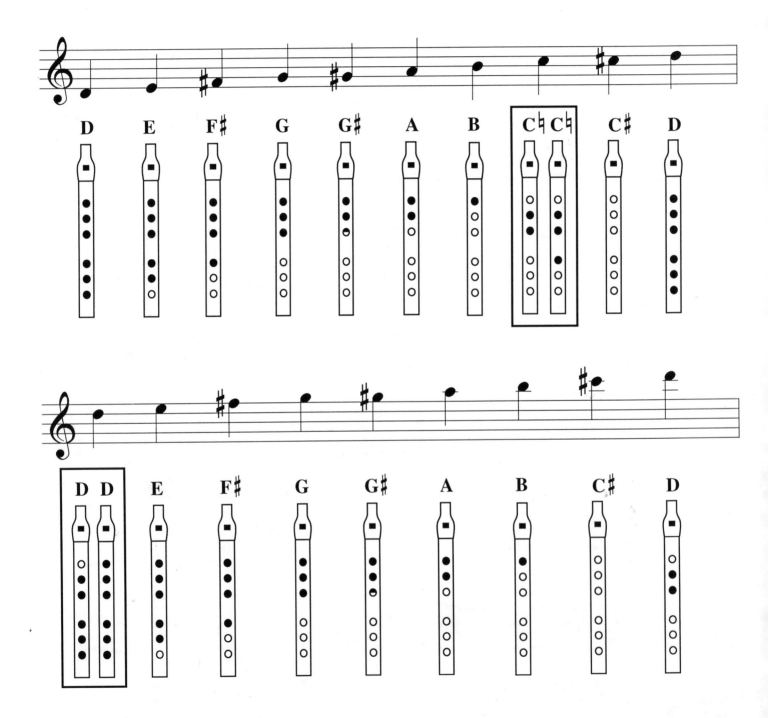